"Good boys and good girls always listen.
To learn we must listen. We must listen all the time.
Good boys and good girls never talk, but they always listen.
We should listen and listen and listen!"
To you, Teacher, and your words, your words, your words.
Your words, your words, your words, your words, your words!

3

It's September again --
Not breathing --
Shivering!
As far from your desk as I can get --
Pretending I'm not here --
Hoping you won't call on me!

You, my dear Teacher, you who tell me my thoughts are wrong.
You who are so neat and strong,
you so strict and proper.
It's as if you can see right through me.
You tell me that I can't and that I shouldn't.
But you, you -- who are you?

DEDICATED TO EVERY GROWNUP WHO, AS A CHILD, DIED IN THE ARMS OF COMPULSORY EDUCATION.

THE GERANIUM ON THE WINDOWSILL
JUST DIED
BUT TEACHER
YOU WENT RIGHT ON

A Harlin Quist Book

Pictures by
Gérard Failly
(Pages 3, 4, 5, 16, 17, 28, 29, 32)
Gilles Bachelet
(Page 6)
Victoria Chess
(Page 9)
Slug Signarino
(Page 11)
Elwood Smith
(Page 13)
Dan Long
(Page 15)
François Roca
(Page 18)
Guy Billout
(Page 21)
Patrick Couratin
(Page 23)
Philippe Weisbecker
(Page 25)
Claude Lapointe
(Page 27)
Nicole Claveloux
(Page 30)
Cover illustration by
Philippe Weisbecker

Published by Harlin Quist Books
63, boulevard de Ménilmontant 75011 Paris, France
Copyright © 1971 by Harlin Quist
Copyright renewed © 1999 by Harlin Quist
Printed in Belgium
ISBN : 0-8252-0500-X

I was good at everything until I started being here with you.
I was good at laughing, playing dead, being king!
Honest, I was good at everything!
And now?
Now I'm only good at everything
on Saturdays and Sundays...

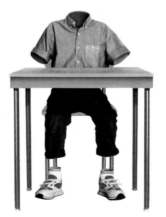

Where is my place in your puzzle, Teach?
Do I fit?
Or am I one piece too many?
Tell me for real, Teach!
I know there's no room for me on your bulletin board,
but do I have a place in your puzzle?...

Of course your classroom is not a circus!
Of course you have rules we have to follow!
Of course there's lots of stuff we must learn!
But, Teacher, can't you smile when you tell us all this?

I have a messy desk.
I have milk money that rolls.
I have a lazy pencil, a book that won't open, a mouth that whispers.
I have a hand that throws crayons, and homework that won't work.
My shirt is out, my shoelaces won't tie,
and sometimes I wet my pants -
but never on purpose.

When you don't like me, Teacher,
I feel the whole world sees me in my underwear,
with no pants on.
I know I'm not very clever.
And sometimes I laugh when I shouldn't.
But I don't want to go home with you not liking me.
Please choose me to water your plants
or clean your blackboard.
Please!

You don't have to call me to your desk.
You don't have to whisper, "For shame! For shame!"
You don't have to send me out in the hallway.
Just tell me that my zipper is open!

I sit in the first row, last seat. I feel you like me.
I mind and I am never late.
Do you like me?
I always do all of my homework,
and I gave you the biggest Valentine of all.
Do you like me?
Sometimes I'm scared of you though.
The way you look, the way you smile,
the way you talk to the other kids.
But that's when you like me best of all - when I'm scared.

You're so proud of your shiny new car.
You're so proud of your new color hair,
your vacation tan,
and your nice clean blackboards.
I sit in the third row, second seat.
Teacher, are you ever proud of me?

Yes, Mr. Principal, I heard what you said.
You don't have to tell me again.
Arf, you are always right.
Arf, you are very great.
Arf, arf, you are God!
Arf, arf... arf.

Your perfume covers the whole room,
but I don't like its smell.
You always tell me that I'm the best,
but sometimes I wish I wasn't.
Teacher, please don't be so nice to me!
Do I have to be your favorite?

It was great seeing you on Saturday.
You said "hello" to me in the center of town.
Even after you passed me, I heard your "hello."
Teacher, does this mean that I'm going to be promoted?
That I can be myself from now on?

You're doing it again, Teacher.
You talk like a train engine or a running tap --
hurry, hurry, hurry, rush, rush, rush!
I get confused.
Can't you slow down?
I don't even know what the question is.

Oh, clean school wall, hallway wall, hold me up!
She pushed me out.
Oh, quiet school wall, hallway wall,
she pushed me hard.
Oh, alone school wall, hallway wall, be my friend!...

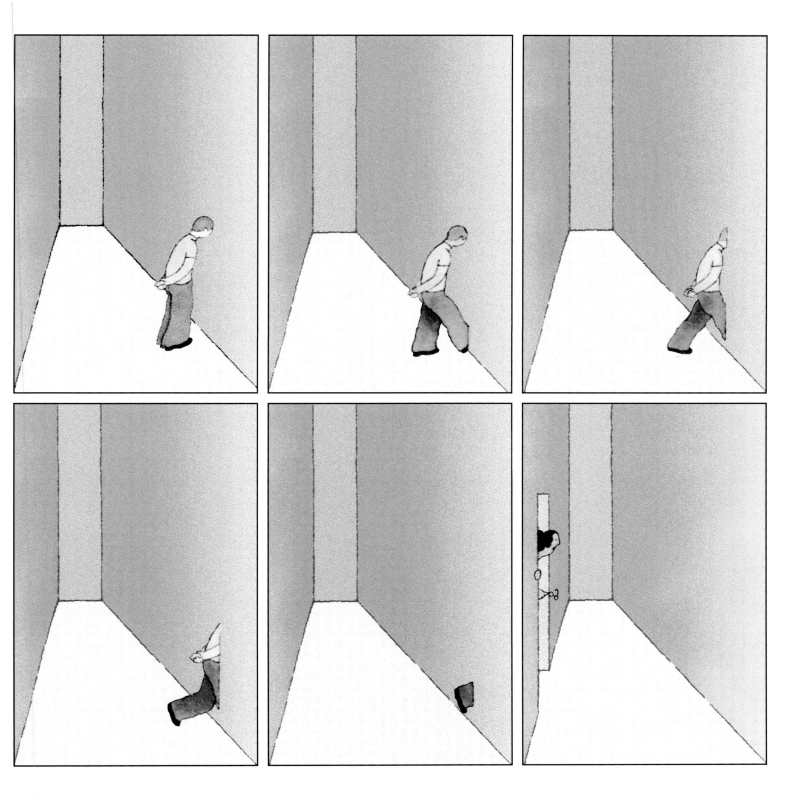

Don't you see my rainbow, Teacher?
Don't you see all the colors?
I know that you're mad at me.
I know you said to color the cherries red and the leaves green.
I know I shouldn't have done it backwards.
But, Teacher, don't you see my rainbow?
Don't you see all the colors?
Don't you see me?

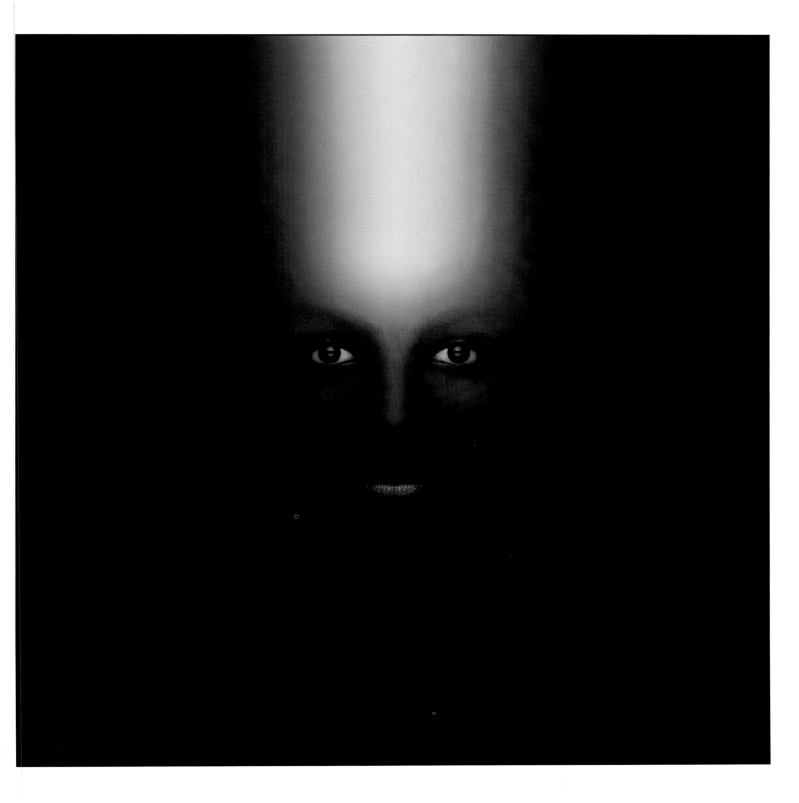

I couldn't help it!
I tried to hold it back!
I tried hard!
I couldn't help it that I farted!
Everyone giggled except you.
You gave me a dirty look.
Why didn't you smile if you've forgotten how to laugh?
At least until the redness went out of my face.

I know it's just a game.
I know it's supposed to be fun, this after-school stuff.
But it isn't.
"Keep at it," you tell me, "be a man."
Well, I'm a kid!

I want you to come to our house, Teach, and yet I don't.
You're so important, but our back door has a hole in it.
And my mother has no fancy cake to serve.
I want you to come to our house, Teacher, and yet I don't.
My brother chews with his mouth open, and sometimes my dad burps.
I wish I could trust you enough, Teacher, to invite you to my house.

You talk funny when you talk to grownups.
And when the teacher next door borrows some paper.
And when my mother comes to visit, you talk funny.
Suddenly, when my mom is here,
I'm your "little princess."
Why don't you talk to them like you talk to us?

Teacher, let me swim in a puddle!
Let me race a cloud across the sky!
Let me build a house without a single wall!
Let me leap, let me whirl, let me fly!...
"Turn to page sixty-seven," you say,
"paragraph two."

Yikes! You scare me when you ask a question
and I don't know the answer.
You always just repeat the question, over and over and over.
But I'm done being scared. You know why?
'Cuz this is my last day in your class
and I don't have to listen to your questions ever again!

"This will be your last day in my class.
I did all that I could to prepare you for the future.
I hope you have learned something.
Does anyone have any questions?...
None?... Good.
Class dismissed."

Teacher, push back the desk and come outside!
I'll race you to the swings!
Don't be afraid, Teacher.
Just grab my hand and follow me.
You can learn all over again!